Theo von Taane

Notebook

Dolphin

Bibliografische Information der Deutschen Nationalbibliothek:
Die Deutsche Nationalbibliothek verzeichnet diese Publikation in der Deutschen Nationalbibliografie; detaillierte bibliografische Daten sind im Internet über http://dnb.dnb.de abrufbar.

© 2016 Text & Covergraphic & Illustrations Theo von Taane;
1. Auflage

Herstellung und Verlag: BoD – Books on Demand, Norderstedt

ISBN: 9783739229805

Books of Theo von Taane

book	ISBN / order nr.
Minecraft Notebook Ender Dragon	9783739228761
Football note- and tactic book	9783734749605
Baseball note- and tactic book	9783734749650
Basketball note- and tactic book	9783734749681
Cricket note- and tactic book	9783734749711
Ice Hockey note- and tactic book	9783734749728
Field Hockey note- and tactic book	9783734749810
Football (Soccer) note- and tactic book	9783734749827
Futsal note- and tactic book	9783734749834
Handball note- and tactic book	9783734749841
Lacrosse Women note- and tactic book	9783734749858
Lacrosse Men note- and tactic book	9783734749865
Netball note- and tactic book	9783734749872
Rugby note- and tactic book	9783734749889
Chess note- and tactic book	9783734749896
Squash note- and tactic book	9783734749902
Tennis note- and tactic book	9783734749919
Table Tennis note- and tactic book	9783734749926
Volleyball note- and tactic book	9783734749933
Water Polo note- and tactic book	9783734749940

Majestic Flowers and Butterflies
- Adult Coloring Book - ISBN: 9783739227085

This coloring book for adults contains 36 beautiful patterns of various flowers. Experience hours full stress relief, mindful calm, creative expression and fun.

Use crayons, felt-tip pens and colored pencils to give the patterns a personal touch.

Millions of people worldwide have rediscovered the simple relaxation and joy of coloring!

Join this community and find yourself enchanted by the magical passion of inspiring coloring.